CAMP PINING PLAY

STEVEN UNIVERSE: CAMP PINING PLAY, April 2019. Published by KaBOOM!, a division of Boom Entertainment, Inc. STEVEN UNIVERSE, CARTOON NETWORK, the logos, and all related characters and elements are trademarks of and © Cartoon Network. A WarnerMedia Company. All rights reserved. (S19) All rights reserved. KaBOOM!™ and the KaBOOM! Logo are trademarks of Boom Entertainment, Inc., registered in various countries and categories. All characters, events, and/or institutions depicted herein are fictional. Any similarity between any of the names, characters, persons, events, and/or institutions in this publication to actual names, characters, and persons, whether living or dead, events and/or institutions is unintended and purely coincidental. KaBOOM! Does not read or accept unsolicited submissions of ideas, stories, or artwork.

For information regarding the CPSIA on this printed material, call: (203) 595-3636 and provide reference #RICH - 825784.

BOOM! Studios, 5670 Wilshire Boulevard, Suite 400, Los Angeles, CA 90036-5679. Printed in USA. First Printing.

ISBN: 978-1-68415-340-4, eISBN: 978-1-64144-193-3

CN CARTOON NETWORK
STEVEN ★ UNIVERSE
CAMP PINING PLAY

created by
REBECCA SUGAR

written by
NICOLE MANNINO

illustrated by
LISA STERLE

colored by
NIMALI ABEYRATNE

lettered by
MIKE FIORENTINO

cover by
FRANCESCA PERRONE

designer
CHELSEA ROBERTS

assistant editor
MICHAEL MOCCIO

editor
MATTHEW LEVINE

With Special Thanks to
Marisa Marionakis, Janet No, Becky M. Yang, Conrad Montgomery,
Jackie Buscarino and the wonderful folks at Cartoon Network.

"YOU SAVED ME," PIERRE SAID THROUGH STRUGGLED BREATHS. WATER WAS DRIPPING DOWN HIS FACE. HIS HAIR WAS MATTED WET, BUT SOMETHING BEHIND HIS DEEP, BROWN EYES GLITTERED.

PERCY GRITTED HIS TEETH. "WHY DIDN'T YOU, LIKE, LISTEN TO PAULETTE WHEN SHE TRIED TO STOP YOU? DUDE...YOU SHOULDN'T EVEN HAVE BEEN ON THE DOCK IN THIS, LIKE, GNARLY WEATHER. YOU COULD'VE, LIKE, GOTTEN HURT!"

PIERRE LOOKED AWAY AND CLENCHED HIS FIST. HIS EXPRESSION WAS A MIXTURE OF HURT AND SOMETHING ELSE THAT PERCY COULDN'T PUT HIS FINGER ON. "I COULDN'T JUST SIT AROUND. I HAD TO DO SOMETHING. YOU..." PIERRE'S VOICE TRAILED OFF.

HE SLOWLY RELAXED HIS HAND, OPENING IT AND REVEALING A SINGLE PUKA SHELL. "YOU WERE SO SAD WHEN YOUR FAVORITE NECKLACE BROKE. I KNEW THE MISSING PUKA SHELL FELL INTO THE LAKE. SO, I HAD TO FIND IT. NO MATTER WHAT," PIERRE SAID.

PERCY CLASPED PIERRE'S HANDS IN HIS AND SHOOK HIS HEAD. "THANKS, DUDE...BUT I'M, LIKE, JUST HAPPY YOU'RE SAFE. YOU'RE, LIKE, WAY MORE IMPORTANT TO ME THAN MY NECKLACE. BECAUSE..." HE SAID, HIS VOICE TRAILING OFF BUT FILLED WITH AFFECTION.

PERCY'S EYES GLISTENED. "PIERRE..."

WAIT!

I WANT THE LAST SCENE OF THIS *"FANFICTION"* TO BE PERFECT.

LAPIS, READ THE CLOSING LINE IN YOUR *"PERCY"* VOICE.

WHAT? NO WAY!

PLEASE! PLEASE, PLEASE, *PLEASE!*

OH, STOP THAT! ALRIGHT...

--IT BECAME AN ACTUAL EPISODE? HAHA!

JUST KIDDING--

YES!

THAT'S A BRILLIANT IDEA!

LET'S MAKE THIS A REALITY!

HOW DO WE ACCOMPLISH THIS?

WHAT IF I CONTACT PERCY, PIERRE, AND PAULETTE RIGHT NOW AND DEMAND THAT THEY MAKE THIS AN EPISODE?

WE CAN USE...STUFFED ANIMALS!

WE CAN USE...FOUND OBJECTS!

OK, WAIT! I'VE GOT A GOOD IDEA, FOR REAL!

LET'S...

...PUT ON A PLAY!

HEH, GOOD ONE, PERIDOT.

HEY, HEY! I'M SERIOUS ABOUT THIS ONE!

OH...

RIGHT...I MEAN, I GUESS IT'S A PRETTY GOOD IDEA. BUT...

DON'T YOU THINK IT'D BE A LOT OF WORK? IT SOUNDS HARD.

IF YOU'RE REALLY SERIOUS ABOUT DOING THIS, WE CAN'T JUST TAKE SOMEONE ELSE'S WORK AND MAKE IT OUR OWN.

HM. YOU PROPOSE A GOOD POINT, LAPIS. HOWEVER, I PROPOSE ONE EVEN BETTER.

WE ASK THE WRITER FOR PERMISSION TO MAKE A PLAY OUT OF THEIR *"FANFICTION"*!

I JUST SIMPLY INPUT ALL THE DESIRED CRITERIA, AND...

FIND-A-CLOD

SEARCH WITHIN:
24,901 MILE RADIUS

LOOKING FOR SOMEONE WHO:

• DESIRES TO BE LOVED AND ACCEPTED
• PROBABLY ONLY HAS 1 FRIEND
• WORKS MINIMAL HOURS AT PART-TIME JOB
• PROBABLY DOESN'T GET HUGGED VERY OFTEN

SEARCH

PING!

FIND-A-CLOD

OH? THAT'S...

INTERESTING.

YOU HAVE FOUND YOUR CLOD(S)!

NAME: Laramie Barriga

SPECIES: clod

LOCATION: Beach City

OCCUPATION: donut butler

GREETINGS, DONUT BUTLER!

ARE YOU THE AUTHOR OF THE HIT *CAMP PINING HEARTS* **"FANFICTION"** THAT IS CALLED CAMPERS' PINING HEARTS (OR: A STORY OF FRIENDSHIP AND LOVE)?

PFFF

WH-WHAT ARE YOU TALKING ABOUT!? F-F-FANFICTION!?

YEAH, RIGHT!

I MEAN, *NO!* NEVER!

OUR VERY THOROUGH, INCREDIBLY SCIENTIFIC CALCULATIONS LEAD US TO BELIEVE THAT YOU ARE USERNAME XX54D4ND1ONE1YXX, AUTHOR OF OVER 30 *CAMP PINING HEARTS* "*FAN-FICTIONS*", NONE OF WHICH ARE POPULAR, EXCEPT FOR THE MOST RECENT AND LONGEST-RUNNING "CHAPTERED" "*FAN-FICTION*" ENTITLED *CAMPERS' PINING HEARTS (OR: A STORY OF FRIENDSHIP AND LOVE)*, WHICH HAS RECENTLY BECOME VIRAL WITHIN THE COMMUNITY.

I SAID *NO!* THAT'S DEFINITELY... DEFINITELY *NOT* ME!

PERHAPS YOU REQUIRE AN EXCERPT TO JOG YOUR MEMORY. AHEM.

CHAPTER 1: CAMP BEGINNINGS. PERCY DROPPED HIS BAG IN THE DOORWAY OF HIS CABIN. HE TOOK A DEEP BREATH, SOAKING IN THE SCENT OF SUMMER--

STOP!

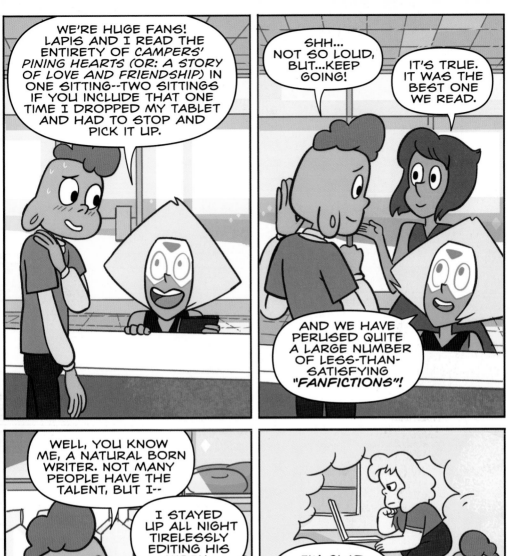

WE'RE HUGE FANS! LAPIS AND I READ THE ENTIRETY OF *CAMPERS' PINING HEARTS (OR: A STORY OF LOVE AND FRIENDSHIP)* IN ONE SITTING--TWO SITTINGS IF YOU INCLUDE THAT ONE TIME I DROPPED MY TABLET AND HAD TO STOP AND PICK IT UP.

SHH... NOT SO LOUD, BUT...KEEP GOING!

IT'S TRUE. IT WAS THE BEST ONE WE READ.

AND WE HAVE PERUSED QUITE A LARGE NUMBER OF LESS-THAN-SATISFYING *"FANFICTIONS"*!

WELL, YOU KNOW ME, A NATURAL BORN WRITER. NOT MANY PEOPLE HAVE THE TALENT, BUT I--

I STAYED UP ALL NIGHT TIRELESSLY EDITING HIS WORK.

I'M GLAD YOU ENJOYED THE STORY. HE WAS NERVOUS ABOUT EVERY CHAPTER HE PUBLISHED.

I WASN'T!

ANYWAY, LAPIS AND I ARE HERE ON BUSINESS. WILL YOU OR WILL YOU NOT ALLOW US TO PERFORM A PLAY BASED ON YOUR STORY?

I SUPPOSE, SINCE IT'S PRETTY MUCH IMPOSSIBLE TO FIND TALENT AS RAW AS THIS.

WHO AM I TO DENY THE WORLD OF SUCH FINE ART--

HE'S OK WITH IT.

HEY!

ALRIGHT, HERE'S THE DEAL.

I'LL LET YOU DO A PLAY ABOUT MY FIC, *IF* YOU LET ME OVERSEE ALL ITS PROGRESS AS AN IN-HOUSE CRITIC TYPE OF THING. AND...

...DON'T ATTACH MY NAME TO THE PROJECT! I GOTTA KEEP UP MY IMAGE, YOU GOT THAT?

I *CAN'T* LET THE COOL KIDS KNOW!

AFFIRMATIVE, DONUT BUTLER!

WHAT DO WE DO, NOW THAT WE HAVE LARS' PERMISSION?

DO ANY OF YOU KNOW HOW TO PUT ON A PLAY?

I MAY REQUIRE YOUR ASSISTANCE WITH THIS PERFORMANCE, DONUT MASTER. WE'LL FARE BETTER WITH A KNOWLEDGEABLE HUMAN COLLABORATOR.

SURE! I'D LOVE TO HELP.

I'LL COME WITH YOU.

W-WAIT, DON'T LEAVE ME HERE ALONE! I'M HELPING, TOO!

1) TALK TO MAYOR DEWEY

UHM...I--I DON'T KNOW, KIDS.

2) HIRE ACTORS AND A CREW

LET US COMMENCE OUR FIRST ORDER OF BUSINESS: CAST AND CREW!

SINCE WE'RE THE MASTER-MINDS BEHIND THIS ENDEAVOR, WE GET DIBS ON PARTS WE'LL BE PLAYING.

I, FOR ONE, WILL BE THE DIRECTOR. I'VE GOT BIG DREAMS FOR THIS PLAY, AND I WISH TO COMMAND EVERYONE TO DO MY BIDDING! NYEHEHEH!

I ALREADY MENTIONED IT BEFORE, BUT I JUST WANNA BE THE IN-HOUSE CRITIC. DON'T CREDIT ME!

I'D BE PERFECTLY HAPPY AS A BACKGROUND CHARACTER.

I'M...I'M NOT SURE IF THERE'S REALLY A CHARACTER THAT FITS ME.

CORRECT. THAT'S WHY THE PART'S PERFECT FOR YOU.

YEAH, THE PART'S PERFECT FOR YOU, LAPIS!

YOU'RE BY FAR THE COOLEST ONE HERE.

HEY!

WELL... I GUESS I'LL TRY IT.

YES!

AAHH!!

AHH!!

SO, UHM...GOOD MORNING, PERIDOT.

WHAT ARE YOU DOING HERE?

I'M GLAD YOU ASKED, STEVEN.

I HAVE A TASK OF UTMOST IMPORTANCE THAT I MUST ASSIGN TO YOU.

AS YOU KNOW, I'M A BIG-- NAY, *COLOSSAL*--FAN OF THE HUMAN TELEVISION FRANCHISE *CAMP PINING HEARTS*. THAT BEING SAID, LAPIS AND I ARE CURRENTLY PUTTING TOGETHER A PLAY BASED ON OUR FAVORITE FAN-CREATED STORY WHICH, BY THE WAY, MIGHT AS WELL BE CANON, BUT I DIGRESS.

TIME ALLOTTED: ONE WEEK UNTIL PERFORMANCE.

CURRENT MISSION: CASTING CALL AND AUDITIONS.

MY QUESTION TO YOU IS...

YO, LIKE, WHAT'S GOIN' ON HERE?

PERIDOT AND LAPIS ARE PUTTING ON A PLAY BASED ON A *CAMP PINING HEARTS* FANFIC WRITTEN BY--

--HOOBA JOOBA HNNF!

WELL...IF IT'S FOR STEVEN, I *SUPPOSE* WE COULD DO THAT.

OHH, THIS IS ABOUT THE SHOW THAT STEVEN LOVES?

LET'S ALL AUDITION!

WOW! THAT WAS SO BEAUTIFUL!

WHY, THANK YOU--

OUTTA THE WAY, NERDS!

LEMME SHOW YOU HOW A *REAL* AUDITION IS DONE.

MORE AUDITIONS!

UHM... LARS?

YOU KNOW, WE DID HAVE FIRST DIBS ON THE CHARACTERS. IF YOU REALLY WANNA PLAY SOMEONE, ALL YOU HAVE TO DO IS ASK.

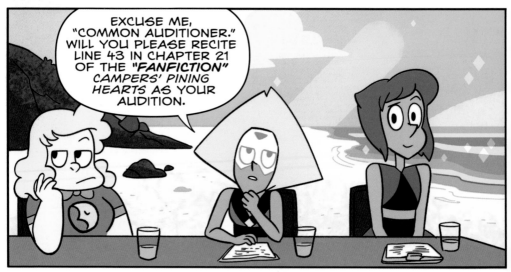

EXCUSE ME, "COMMON AUDITIONER." WILL YOU PLEASE RECITE LINE 43 IN CHAPTER 21 OF THE *"FANFICTION"* CAMPERS' PINING HEARTS AS YOUR AUDITION.

LARS HAS NOTHING TO DO WITH THIS!

3) MAKE PROPS

CONGRATULATIONS ON MAKING IT PAST THE AUDITION STAGE, RESIDENT CLODS!

AS YOUR REWARD, I WILL DUTIFULLY ANNOUNCE THAT WE CURRENTLY HAVE EXACTLY 2¢ IN FUNDS TO CREATE PROPS FOR THIS MAGNIFICENTLY BRILLIANT PLAY.

YOU, AS SIMPLE BEINGS, MAY ASSUME THAT'S A BAD THING. HOWEVER--

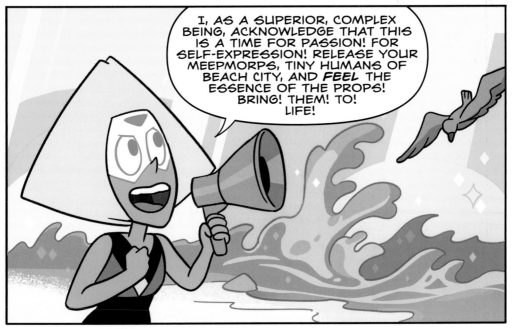

I, AS A SUPERIOR, COMPLEX BEING, ACKNOWLEDGE THAT THIS IS A TIME FOR PASSION! FOR SELF-EXPRESSION! RELEASE YOUR MEEPMORPS, TINY HUMANS OF BEACH CITY, AND *FEEL* THE ESSENCE OF THE PROPS! BRING! THEM! TO! LIFE!

IF YOU WANT TO BE IN THIS PLAY, PLEASE GET TO WORK ON BUILDING CAMP-LIKE PROPS FOR OUR PLAY. OTHERWISE, YOU CAN LEAVE.

HM, YES,
I SEE.

OH,
HM, OK.

OHHHHHHH,
YES, YES.

I'VE GOT AN IDEA!

I'LL COMPILE A LIST OF REQUIRED, *USEFUL* PROPS. IF ANYONE OWNS ANY OF THE ITEMS NECESSARY, WE CAN SIMPLY USE *THOSE* AS OUR PROPS!

AH, YES... THIS LOOKS COMPLETE.

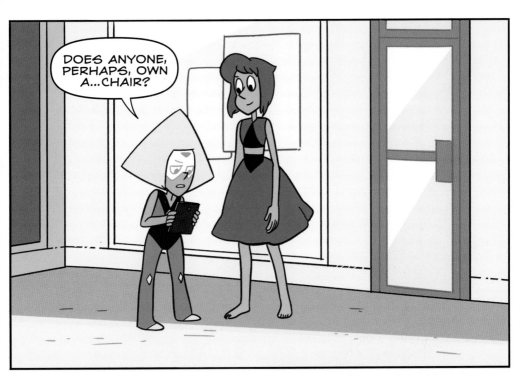

DOES ANYONE, PERHAPS, OWN A...CHAIR?

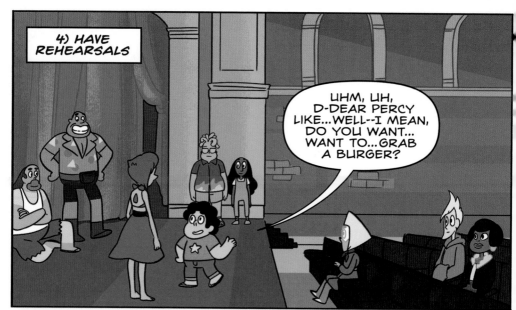

4) HAVE REHEARSALS

UHM, UH, D-DEAR PERCY LIKE...WELL--I MEAN, DO YOU WANT... WANT TO...GRAB A BURGER?

CUT!

STEVEN! LIKE I SAID THE LAST 2 TIMES. THE LINE IS *NOT* "WANT TO GRAB A BURGER"!

IT'S "WHAT'S WRONG, PERCY"!

BOOOOO!

I'M SORRY, PERIDOT. PLEASE LET ME TRY AGAIN!

I PROMISE I'LL GET IT RIGHT THIS TIME.

PROCEED, STEVEN.

AHEM.

HEYYY, PERCY, MY MAN! DO YOU... DO YOU...WANT TO...GRAB A BURGER?

LAPIS! WILL YOU PLEASE DO THE HONOR OF SHOWING STEVEN HOW IT'S DONE?

OH! UHM... I-I'M...

WE SHOULD LET THE MUSICIANS PRACTICE! AFTER ALL, THE MUSIC WILL BE PLAYING THROUGHOUT THE ENTIRETY OF THE PLAY.

AH, YES! REQUEST GRANTED.

HA!

I, PENELOPE, HAVE WON THE WHEELBARROW RACE!

AND NOW, FOR MY PRIZE.

HAND OVER THE PUKA SHELL NECKLACE YOU VICIOUSLY STOLE FROM PERCY, PARKER!

CUT!

FIRST OFF, CONNIE, REGARDLESS OF THE FACT THAT WE'RE USING A WHEELBARROW AND A TRASHCAN, IT'S STILL TECHNICALLY A *CANOE* RACE.

PLEASE USE YOUR TINY BRAIN'S IMAGINATION MORE EFFICIENTLY.

AND ONION, I IMPLORE YOU *NOT* TO DEVIATE FROM THE SCRIPT!

THAT WAS ALSO OUR *ONLY* PUKA SHELL NECKLACE.

YOU RANG?

HA! I, PENELOPE, HAVE WON THE WHEELBARROW RACE!

AND NOW, FOR MY PRIZE.

HAND OVER THE PUKA SHELL NECKLACE YOU VICIOUSLY STOLE FROM PERCY, PARKER!

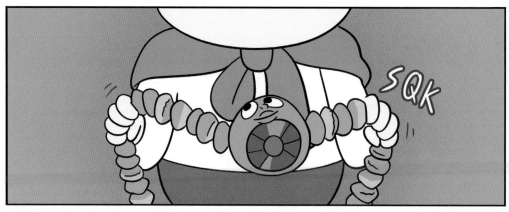

HIGHLY IMPRESSIVE, AMETHYST!

I MUST ADMIT, MAYBE YOU DO HAVE IT IN YOU TO SAVE THE DAY!

BOOOOO!

I'M DOING MY BEST TO COMPLETE THIS JOB THAT HAS BEEN ASSIGNED TO ME, ESPECIALLY SINCE STEVEN--WHO'S DOING GREAT, BY THE WAY--LOVES THE SHOW THIS PLAY IS BASED ON BUT... QUITE HONESTLY, I'M JUST NOT SURE.

AND, FROM THE LOOKS OF IT...

...PERCY AND PIERRE AREN'T SURE, EITHER.

I'M ALSO NOT FEELING IT.

CONNIE?

PEARL IS RIGHT. THIS PLAY DOESN'T FEEL LIKE US, AND THAT'S WHY WE'RE STRUGGLING!

MAYBE WE CAN MAKE THIS PLAY SOMETHING THAT'S OUR OWN?

AND, IF PERCY AND PIERRE ARE LACKING CHEMISTRY, MAYBE WE CAN WORK WITH SOMETHING THEY CAN DO?

MAYBE... MAYBE PERCY AND PIERRE CAN FUSE!

WAIT, CONNIE, FUSION IS--

--SOMETHING DEEP AND PER-SONAL, NOT A STAGE TRICK.

OBJECTION!

HUH?

ATTENTION, CLODS! I'VE COME TO A DECISION!

SO...

TOMORROW'S THE BIG DAY...

OPENING DAY.

YEAH. IT FEELS LIKE JUST YESTERDAY, THAT I--

"--MADE A TYPING ERROR WHILE SEARCHING UP THE *CAMP PINING HEARTS* WEBSITE,

"UNKNOWINGLY CLICKED ON A FAN WEBSITE BY ACCIDENT,

IS IT ME OR MY HEART THAT'S RACING?
Based on the fic CPH(o:aSoF&L)

"SAW A FASCINATING FANART FOR A *"FANFICTION"*,

MY HEART RACING?

CPH(o:a   &L)

"INVESTIGATED SAID *"FANFICTION"*,

"PERUSED THE *"FANFICTION"* IN ITS ENTIRETY,

"AND THEN, ULTIMATELY, DETERMINED TO CREATE A PLAY BASED ON IT."

I'M WORRIED THAT I'LL MESS EVERYTHING UP FOR EVERYONE.

WHAT!? NO WAY!

IN THE BEGINNING, I WANTED EVERYTHING TO BE PERFECT.

BUT THE MORE STEVEN REQUESTED LINE CHANGES, THE MORE MONOLOGUES CONNIE SUBJECTED US TO ABOUT FREEDOM OF CHOICE, AND AS TIME PROGRESSED, I REALIZED THAT...

EVEN THOUGH IT FEELS REALLY GOOD TO FOLLOW THE RULES AND DO EVERYTHING RIGHT, MAYBE... MAYBE...

HAVING FUN WITH YOUR FRIENDS IS THE MOST IMPORTANT PART...?

THAT SOUNDS CONVINCING.

I'M SERIOUS!! I'M STILL LEARNING, TOO!

I KNOW.

PLUS, SHOULDN'T WE CHANNEL THE HEART AND PASSION THAT'S SO SUCCESSFULLY EMBODIED IN *CAMP PINING HEARTS*?

WHAT A GRAVE ERROR WE'D COMMIT IF WE DIDN'T AT LEAST PRETEND TO LIVE AS WILDLY AS OUR BELOVED CHARACTERS!

PERHAPS THIS IS OUR TRUE INITIATION INTO THEIR WORLD--A TEST FROM THE POWERS THAT GAVE US PERCY, PIERRE--

STOP THAT!

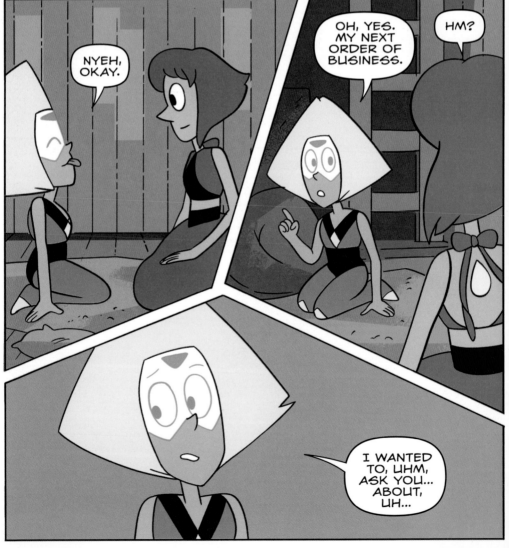

I WANTED TO ASK ABOUT THE FAKE FUSION SCENE YOU HAVE WITH STEVEN.

I KNOW IT'S A FAKE FUSION, BUT...

ARE YOU OK WITH IT?

YOU DON'T HAVE TO--

I'M FINE WITH IT.

IT'S JUST LIKE YOU SAID, IT'S A FAKE FUSION.

I MEAN, WE DID JUST DISCUSS HAVING CREATIVE LIBERTY, I'M SURE STEVEN AND CONNIE WOULD *LOVE* TO REWRITE--

IT'S FINE.

"I COULD, LIKE, NEVER FORGET THE LANGUAGE OF MY HEART, PAULETTE."

BRILLIANT! INCREDIBLE! DAZZLING!

YOU TRY DOING THE VOICE.

"OK, LIKE, PERHAPS YOUR PARTNERSHIP INSPIRES A POSITIVE CHANGE WITHIN MY THOUGHT PROCESS, PIERRE."

WHEN DID PERCY EVER SAY THAT?

I WANTED TO, UHM, ACKNOWLEDGE THE AMOUNT OF HARD WORK AND EFFORT EVERYONE EXERTED IN ORDER TO SUCCESSFULLY COMPLETE THIS PLAY.

I STRONGLY BELIEVE WE ACCOMPLISHED THE TASK SET BEFORE US: TO TAKE AN INSPIRING STORY AND BRING IT TO LIFE BY USING NOTHING BUT OUR BLOOD, SWEAT, TEARS, AND OBJECTS FROM HOME.

WE STARTED WITH NOTHING BUT OUR RESOLVE AND ENDED WITH A PLAY THAT COMPLETELY DISREGARDS ITS SOURCED WORK AND, FRANKLY, HAS ALMOST BECOME AN ENTIRELY DIFFERENT STORY IN THE END BUT, HEY, IT'S ABOUT THE HEART, RIGHT? THE CAMP PINING HEART! *HA!*

BUT, I DIGRESS, BECAUSE WE ACCEPTED OUR MISSION AND COMPLETELY TOOK CONTROL OF IT!

OF COURSE, IT WOULD BE NEAR IMPOSSIBLE TO GET AS FAR AS WE DID WITHOUT MY EXPERTISE. AM I RIGHT? OR AM I RIGHT?

NYEHEH! ANYWAY.

IN THE WORDS OF PERCY: "IT'S ABOUT, LIKE, THE HALFWAY DECENT ACQUAINTANCES WE MADE ALONG THE WAY."

HE NEVER SAID THAT.

SO, IN CONCLUSION--

I HAD A LOT OF FUN WITH YOU CLODS.

I THANK YOU, ALL.

ESPECIALLY...

DONUT MASTER AND, OF COURSE, DONUT BUTLER, WHO, SINCE THE BEGINNING--

I HAD ABSOLUTELY *NOTHING* TO DO WITH THIS!

NOTED.

AND, UHM...

IF I LEARNED ANYTHING FROM *CAMP PINING HEARTS*, IT'S...

THAT THERE'S SUBSTANTIAL STRENGTH IN PARTNERSHIPS.

SO THANK YOU FOR BEING MY PARTNER IN THIS, LAPIS.

WE BEGIN OUR STORY OF FRIENDSHIP AND LOVE WITH THE MOVING TALE ON WHEN...

PERCY LEFT MY GRASP.

HEY, PAULETTE.

DO YOU KNOW WHERE PERCY IS? WE'RE SUPPOSED TO GO OUT TO-- UH...

BUT I WISH HE WAS HERE!

HEY, DON'T WORRY.

IT'S JUST LIKE PERIDOT SAID EARLIER! IT'S THE HEART OF THE PLAY THAT MATTERS.

WE'RE JUST HERE TO HAVE FUN.

RIGHT...

IT'LL BE OK.

ALL OF US ARE HERE TO HELP AND SUPPORT EACH OTHER--AND THAT INCLUDES *YOU*.

WE'VE BEEN WORKING HARD, BUT MOSTLY HAVING FUN. YOU'LL DO GREAT!

RIGHT!

THANK YOU.

SHOVE

AHEM.

I'M, LIKE, TOTALLY HERE, PAULETTE. DID YOU CALL ME, OR WERE WE, LIKE, HAVING AN EMOTIONAL CONNECTION?

I'LL SAVE YOU, PIERRE!

I COULDN'T JUST SIT AROUND AND NOT DO ANYTHING! THIS--

THIS PUKA SHELL IS SO IMPORTANT TO YOU, BECAUSE IT'S FROM YOUR NECKLACE.

AND THAT PUKA SHELL NECKLACE IS EVEN MORE IMPORTANT TO YOU THAN HOW IMPORTANT HAMBURGERS ARE TO ME. THAT'S SAYING A LOT!

I HAD TO SAVE YOUR PRECIOUS ITEM, PERCY!

UH--UHM. RIGHT AS I WAS FALLING INTO THE LAKE, I HEARD PAULETTE YELLING AT YOU NOT TO GO OUT, SINCE IT'S DANGEROUS IN THIS WEATHER.

I THOUGHT NO ONE WOULD FIND ME OUT HERE!

BUT, YOU...YOU CAME FOR ME, PIERRE.

HERE YOU GO, PERCY.

OH... UHM. THANK YOU, PIERRE. YOU'RE-- YOU'RE...

WHAT IS HAPPENING???

UHM...

OH, NO!
OH, NO!

LAPIS...? ARE YOU OK?

LAPIS!

I KNOW IT'S A FAKE FUSION. IT'S NOT EVEN REAL!

SO WHY AM I STILL SO SCARED?

I'M SORRY.

YOU ASKED ME MORE THAN ONCE. I TOLD YOU THAT I WAS FINE WITH THE SCENE.

I WANTED TO BE OK WITH IT.

I WANTED TO HAVE FUN WITH EVERYONE ELSE.

BUT...

I WAS SO WORRIED ABOUT MESSING UP EVERYONE'S FUN, THAT I ENDED UP DOING EXACTLY THAT.

NO.

YOUR UNCOMFORTABILITY DOESN'T RUIN OUR FUN.

EXACTLY!!

AND THE HAPPINESS OF THE GROUP RELIES ON THE INDIVIDUAL! IF YOU'RE HAPPY, WE'LL ALL BE HAPPY!

IT'S *LESS* FUN TO INCLUDE SOMETHING THAT RUINS THE FUN FOR SOMEONE ELSE.

RIGHT, PERIDOT?

OH, UH--YES! YES, THAT'S CORRECT.

YEAH, BUT IT WAS A *FAKE* FUSION. IT WASN'T EVEN REAL.

IT DOESN'T MATTER, REAL OR FAKE, IT'S OK TO BE UNCOMFORTABLE WITH SOMETHING.

AND IF YOU'RE UNCOMFORTABLE, WE DON'T WANT IT.

WHAT'S GOING ON?

THEY'RE DOING IT FOR YOU, LAPIS!

WHAT?

IT APPEARS AS THOUGH EVERYONE ELSE DID THE FUSION SCENE, SO YOU DIDN'T HAVE TO!

Thank you.

THE
END

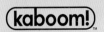